WORDS
TO LIVE BY

*Jim & Lynn,
Many blessings
to you and yours
forever.
Peace! Bob
10/21/12*

ALSO BY
ROBERT TREMMEL

The Four Gospels

WORDS
TO LIVE BY

ROBERT TREMMEL

Copyright © 2012 by Robert Tremmel.

Library of Congress Control Number: 2012915775
ISBN: Hardcover   978-1-4797-0499-6
          Softcover   978-1-4797-0498-9
          Ebook   978-1-4797-0500-9

All rights reserved. No part of this book may be reproduced or transmitted in any form or by any means, electronic or mechanical, including photocopying, recording, or by any information storage and retrieval system, without permission in writing from the copyright owner.

This book was printed in the United States of America.

To order additional copies of this book, contact:
Xlibris Corporation
1-888-795-4274
www.Xlibris.com
Orders@Xlibris.com
120534

TABLE OF CONTENTS

    Acknowledgements...7

    The Text..8

    Foreword...9

    Preface...11

1. Who Do People Say That I Am?..13

2. Acknowledging Our Sins..28

3. Those Who Walk In The Light 43

4. God Does Not Cause Suffering 53

5. Lord, Teach Us To Pray 64

6. Forgiveness Leads To Love...80

7. A Little Bit of Heaven on the Way to Heaven...................94

This book is dedicated to all who seek to better understand the meaning of life as proposed by the Word of Life who is Jesus Christ.

ACKNOWLEDGEMENTS

I am indebted to all those who have encouraged me to write another book and for their suggestions and support. I would particularly like to thank my wife Robbie for her critical review, Sr. Betty Leon, Mary Urbanski, my son Matthew for their valuable input and Deacon Tom Bousamara for writing the Forward. I am blessed to have such wonderful friends and family.

All the biblical quotations used in this book are taken from *The New American Bible*, copyright 1986.

THE TEXT

You will notice that the text used in this book has been divided into clause and phrase units. This practice is known as *per cola et commata*. It was used by the ancient Romans for educational purposes. St. Jerome used it in his translation of the Greek and Hebrew Scriptures into the Latin Vulgate. I have modified the method to suit my own needs so I am not following the strict guidelines incorporated by the Romans.

The first time I saw it in a modern text was a book called *That Man is You*, written by Father Louis Evely. Father Evely, a Belgian Priest, was a spiritual writer in the 1960's and 70's who had a great deal of influence on my spiritual life. I have tried to incorporate Evely's style in this book. While the thoughts and words are quite different, I hope I have captured his ability to retell the Gospel message in a very unique and relevant way.

Per cola et commata allows the writer to isolate certain phrases, clauses and even single words which makes the text, not only appear to be poetic, but also suitable for meditation. Separating the units in the sentence helps the reader to focus on basic thoughts and ideas. I found this helped me to better understand Evely's ideas because certain words and phrases caught my attention, since they stood out, forcing me in a way to take special note of them. It is my hope that it will help you do the same.

Robert Tremmel

FOREWORD

"The unexamined life is not worth living," posited Socrates over 2400 years ago. The boldness of the second half of this short but balanced sentence—that an unreflective, and therefore, unintentional existence has **no value**—has certainly captured the attention of philosophers and other intelligent folks ever since.

For Socrates the purpose of human life was growth, personal and spiritual. Constantly challenging the status quo and those in authority around him, he demonstrated over and over again that unless we take the time to examine and reflect, purpose eludes us. And yet the "how to" of holding up human existence for meaningful examination has puzzled so many otherwise thoughtful people from the dawn of philosophy onward.

For Christians, however, for those with "eyes to see" and "ears to hear", the lens of faith can help us see more clearly our true nature and respond to life with a sense of purpose. All that is needed is a suitable guide to help us glide across the deep pools of scripture, Christology, ecclesiology and all the other "—ologies" that sometimes prevent well-intentioned people from wrestling with the big questions of Christian existence.

One such guide is Deacon Bob Tremmel. In *Words to Live by*, he grapples with the important questions relevant for our times. To mention just a few of these:

- How could Jesus have both human and divine knowledge while on earth? How can an understanding of this human and divine Jesus of scripture and faith help us see the Incarnation continuing in each of us?
- Why is it harmful to highlight sins instead of sinfulness? Why does one lead to legalism and the other to healthier relationships? And where do conscience, grace and humility fit into this more wholesome picture of self?
- Why is there suffering?

- How can we move beyond the small gods we tend to "invent" to make better use of prayer time? Why do we cajole or blame a God who already wants what is best for us even before we address him? How did Jesus pray?
- How does forgiveness lead us to a bit of heaven right here and right now?

In addition to selecting the right questions for our times, Deacon Tremmel helps the reader make these important truths his/her own by phrasing them in a quasi-poetic way. Using the ancient format of *per cola et commata*, important thoughts, phrases and even single words help the reader weigh them and give him or her time to pause and absorb each. The Gospel message not only powers through in this unique and compelling way, but our response, our desire to live a more intentional life, a life given over to the Lord, is engaged as well.

Deacon Tom
Bousamra
May 31, 2012

PREFACE

In my book, "The Four Gospels" I mentioned that I was a member of Saint Roch Catholic community in the 1970's. Ironically, my wife and I recently became members again. The first time I was at Saint Roch I became involved in the neo-Pentecostal movement, otherwise known as the Charismatic Renewal. At the urging of the Pastor, Fr. Val Kasznowski, I started attending charismatic prayer meetings at the Immaculate Heart of Mary motherhouse in Monroe, Michigan. I was amazed, not only by the incredible power of the Holy Spirit, but also by the ecumenical environment of those meetings. There were not just Catholics but Presbyterians, Episcopalians, Methodists, Lutherans and even a few Baptists in attendance. We experienced the phenomenon of speaking in tongues, described by St Paul, as well as miracles and healings. Yet, what impressed me most was people from all walks of life witnessing about the wonderful things Jesus was doing in their lives.

It was at those meetings that I learned God can do anything if we simply allow Him to actively participate in our lives, even bringing several Christian denominations together as one body in Christ! It was there that I learned to read and reflect on the Scriptures by calling on the Holy Spirit for understanding and guidance.

As a result, I believe it is very important to read the Sacred Scriptures, especially the Gospels, for personal edification. I learned in those prayer meetings that, if we open our hearts to the presence of the Holy Spirit, we can encounter God in amazing ways. I can remember countless occasions where I would simply pray for the guidance of the Spirit, open my bible, and passages I had read countless times would almost leap off the pages with insights I had never thought of before. I found this to be invaluable for preparing homilies and classes but it was the application to my personal life that really made a difference.

This book is the product of those encounters; however, I must add that the influence of Louis Evely has also inspired me to write this book. As I mentioned in "The Text", Father Evely opened up new insights into my understanding, not only of the Catholic faith, but also Christianity in general. He had a unique way of saying things. He was down-to-earth but could express truths which were profound. His in-your-face style challenged me and made me think about my faith in many different ways. Most of all he made me want to be a follower of Christ and a lover of Jesus, the Father and the Spirit. Personal relationships with God were not for Catholics, I thought, but Evely made me want to know and love God intimately. His books were a life changing experience.

This book, I'm sure, captures some of Father Evely's thoughts and insights but I have, over the years, been able to homogenize them into my own thoughts about what the Scriptures, particularly the Gospels, are saying. Much of what I have written here I have used in my homilies over the past thirty two years.

Below you will find reflections on the humanity of Jesus and who we are as human beings created in God's image. I have also touched on the nature and meaning of sin perhaps in a way you've never heard before. Other chapters include reflections on suffering, prayer, forgiveness and love. The last chapter is perhaps my favorite because it is about heaven, not so much the heaven we will experience but the heaven we are already experiencing.

This is not a book meant for casual reading nor is it a book to be read quickly. It is a book that should be read, perhaps a chapter at a time, slowly and carefully. These are words for reflection, words that hopefully will make you think more deeply about what it means to be a Catholic and a Christian.

I pray that you will find this little book inspiring and thought provoking. In my wildest dreams, I hope it will inspire you as Louis Evely inspired me although, perhaps that is too much to wish for. At the very least, I hope it will help to bring you closer to God and each other.

CHAPTER ONE

Who Do People Say That I Am?

Now Jesus and his disciples set out for the village of Caesarea Philippi. Along the way he asked his disciples, "Who do people say that I am?" They said in reply, "John the Baptist, others Elijah, still others one of the prophets." And he asked them, "But who do you say that I am? Peter said to him in reply, "You are the Messiah." Then he warned them not to tell anyone about him (Mark 8:27-30).

"Who do people say that I am?"

What a strange question.

Why does Jesus ask this?

Is He taking a survey?

Does He want to find out how popular He is?

Doesn't He know who He is?

Perhaps not!

I say this because many people I know sort of see Jesus as a person who looked like man but was really God inside;

or, He was a perfect human being,
who happened to be divine

or, worse still, God,
who happened to be human.

They never really get it-
>> the pronouncement by the Church at the Council of Nicaea,
>> that Jesus is true God and true man,
>> separate and distinct,
>>>> yet somehow united to only one
>>>> divine person.

Think about this for a moment.

If Jesus were totally God,
>> then He would have known everything.

Everything would have been laid out for Him from the beginning:

>> a blueprint of His life.

He would have known
>> when He would be baptized and by whom.

He would have known
>> when He'd start his public ministry,

>> who He would heal,

>> how many demons He would expel,

>> when He would die
>>>> and that He would be raised from the dead.

If He were only God,
>> who simply appeared to be human,
>>>> He would have known every detail in advance.

Then He would have been no more than an actor on a stage.

Let me ask you, "Did Jesus have faith?"

>> "Why sure," you say, "He was a man of great faith."

Then how can you say He knew everything?

Let me put it another way.

Supposing you knew from the beginning every facet of your life;

> who your parents would be,

> where you'd go to school,

> the names of your friends,

> every time you'd get sick,

> what kind of job you'd have,

> who you'd marry,

> how many children you'd have,

> when you would die

> and when your spouse, children
>> and every loved one would die.

Supposing you knew exactly when God intervened
and how God dealt with everything
that happened in your life.

Would you have faith?

Would you need to have faith?

Faith in what?

Hebrews 11:1 says

> "Faith is the realization of what is hoped for and
> evidence of things not seen."

There's no hope.

Nothing is unseen.

You know everything!

So, if you say, Jesus knew everything,
    then He didn't need to have faith in God.

Yet the Letter to the Hebrews says
    that Jesus can sympathize with our weaknesses
        and was tested in every way (4:15).

    Paul says He was born of a woman (Gal 4:4).

    John 1:14 says the Word became flesh.

    Luke 2:52 says He advanced in wisdom and grace with age.

How can this be?

How can Jesus be "born of a woman",
    be a human being, grow in wisdom and knowledge
        and also be God?

Maybe Jesus was just testing them to see
    if they were really paying attention.

The one who figures it out (Peter in this case)
    gets to be in charge.

Yet, could it be that Jesus wasn't really sure?

Could it be that He needed confirmation from His closest friends
    so that He'd stay the course God had chosen for Him.

After all, there was a Jewish belief that
> when two or more prayerful and godly people
>> agreed on an issue it was a sign it was true.

Remember when Jesus was arrested and tried,
> they couldn't get two people to agree on their testimony (Mk 14:56).

If Jesus were truly a man
> then He would have struggled with life as we do.

He would gradually come to understand the mysteries of life over time.

> "He advanced in wisdom and age and favor . . ."

Naturally, He would bounce His ideas off of His friends,
> especially His closest and most trusted friends.

Don't we do that?

Of course we do!

Why do so many people, Catholics in particular,
> have such a problem with a human Jesus?

The truth is we've always had a problem with the Incarnation.

The Church argued about who Jesus really was for over 300 years!

And then,
> when they finally came up with the notion of true God
> and true man,
>> two natures
>>> hypostatically united to one divine person
>>>> the Church said it was a mystery—incomprehensible!

We don't understand it
> so we hang on to the divine part

    and sort of set aside the human part.

Why?

Because deep down we don't want a God who's human.

Humans have clay feet;
  they make mistakes
    and most of all they can't be trusted.

Did Jesus make mistakes?

He thought the world was flat.

  ". . . you will be my witnesses . . . to the *ends of the earth*"
  (Acts 1:8). Italics mine.

That's just a saying we say.

Yes it is but it's our saying,
  not of the first century Jew or Greek.

For the people of the Greco-Roman world
  it literally meant "the four corners of the earth".

Did Jesus know everything?

He didn't know when the end of the world was coming (Mk 13:32)
  or what His disciples were talking about (Lk 24:17).

Why do we have a problem with a Jesus who is fully human,
  who gets tired,
    and is afraid,
      afraid of being made a king and yes,
        even afraid to die?

Doesn't Jesus tell us
  that it is in weakness we find strength;
    it is in dying that we are reborn?

Doesn't He say the last will be first
        and that we must be the least
                if we are to be the greatest?

What does Paul say?

> "Though he was in the form of God, he did not deem equality with God something to be grasped. Rather he emptied himself, taking the form of a slave, coming in human likeness and found in human appearance, he humbled himself becoming obedient to death, even death on the cross" (Phil 2:6-8).

Paul knew what he was talking about.

He saw Jesus as the new Adam.

> "The first man, Adam, became a living being, the last Adam, a life-giving spirit" (1 Cor 15:45).

The first Adam was created in the image, i.e. form, of God.

> "In the divine image he created them" (Gen 1:27).

But the first Adam wanted to be like God.

The serpent told him and Eve,

> ". . . you will be like gods who know what is good and what is bad" (Gen 3:5).

Jesus, on the other hand, did exactly the opposite.

He didn't desire to be equal to God
        but wanted to be as fully human as possible,
                even to the point of being of lowly estate.

Wow!

Think about that.

Talk about a mystery!

God didn't become a King or the High Priest; not even a Levite.

He became a slave.

In fact, the literal translation is *bondservant*!

And the person He became was very different than the first man
        because, unlike Adam, He obeyed God
                even to the point of death.

"Who do people say that I am?"

"You are the Christ, the Son of the living God," Peter proclaimed.

Oh, Peter you were right on.

        The problem was you had no idea
                what you were talking about!

        "Simon, son of John, flesh and blood has not revealed
        this to you, but my heavenly Father" (Matt 16:17).

Peter is like most of us
        because we have little or no idea
                what we're talking about
                        when we confess who Jesus is.

When Jesus said, ". . . the Son of Man must suffer and die" (Mk 8:31) Peter tried to dissuade him.

        And what did Jesus say to him?

        "Get behind me Satan" (Mk 8:33).

The same guy,
> through whom God just spoke,
>> is now an agent of the Devil!

For sure he didn't know what he was talking about
> when he called Jesus the Messiah.

Still, we can't blame Peter because he's just like us.

Wouldn't we say the same thing?

How could Jesus die, especially at the hands of men?

> He's God!

Can God die?

Apparently, our God can!

All of us believe that Jesus died on the cross don't we?

Actually, a lot of second and third century Christians,
> whom the Church labeled as heretics,
>> said that the divine Jesus not only didn't die
>>> but also couldn't die.

They denied His humanity.

They said Jesus only appeared to be human.

He was a vision, a phantasm.

Others said His divine nature left Him as He hung on the cross.

> "My God, my God why have you abandoned me?"
> (Mk 16:35).

So, for them, only the human Jesus died.

So, you see we're not alone.

People have been struggling with this for centuries.

Millennia!

"Who do you say that I am?"

What a question!

And He's still asking it!

And we're still wondering about the answer.

Oh sure, we say He's divine.

We call Him our savior.

He's the Lord, and as Peter said,

> "The Messiah and the Son of God."

He's all of those things
> but what does it all mean?

> Especially the human part.

Why do you think God decided to become human?

Have you ever seen God?

Is God easy to communicate with?

Easy to understand?

Can we understand quantum mechanics?

> The theory of relativity?

How about the universe?

The vastness of space?

Do you realize that if you were traveling the speed of light, about 186,000 miles a second, which is fast enough to circumnavigate the earth seven times in a second, it would take you 4.5 years to get to the nearest star!

At that incredible speed it would take you 1.5 million years to get to the nearest galaxy and over 13 billion years to get to the furthest known galaxy.

And who do we say made all this;
        is in charge of all this?

We can't even begin to comprehend these numbers.

So how can we understand God?

We have a hard enough time understanding each other!

That's why we have Jesus.

Jesus is a man,
        who is one with the Father,
                who hears the words of the Father.

Do you want to know about God?

        What God is like?

        What God expects from you?

Then read the Gospels.

Do you want to know how to live life?

        What you need to do

                to please God,

  to honor God,

  to serve God?

Do you?

Then read the Gospels.

When we read the Gospels we hear Jesus
  and when Jesus speaks
    God is speaking.

But Jesus is also a man,
  a human being
    and we can relate to human beings.

That's what makes the Incarnation so amazing,
  and so wonderful!

Because Jesus is human,
  He is the perfect model for us
    who are also human.

What a gift the Incarnation is!

Not only because we have the perfect mediator between us and God,
  not only because Jesus reveals God to us in a way
  we can understand,
    but also, because we have been purified by it.

When the Word became flesh all of humanity was able to say,

  "We are sanctified."

  "We are made holy!"

As Jesus was proclaimed "Messiah",
  this means "anointed one",
    so we too are "anointed ones".

We were anointed
> when we were baptized
>> and again when we were confirmed.

The same question Jesus asked His disciples
> can be asked of you and me.

Who do people say you are?

Are you Christ-like in what you say and do?

Are you forgiving?

> "Father, forgive them for they know not what they are doing" (Lk 4:34).

Do you judge others?

> "Stop judging that you may not be judged" (Matt 7:1).

Are you kind and merciful?

> "Blessed are the merciful" (Matt 5:7).

Are you unyielding and overly critical?

> "The measure you use to use to measure others will be measured out to you" (Matt 7:2).

We need not stop here.

The list could go on and on.

The more we read the Gospels,
> the more we know about Jesus
>> and the more we know about God
>>> and what God expects of us.

If we dare to call ourselves Christians
> then we must dare to imitate Christ.

"Follow me" (Mk 1:17) he told Peter, Andrew, James, John
and countless others.

"Sell everything you have and give it to the poor" (Mk 10:21)
He told the rich young man.

"Love one another as I have loved you" (Jn 15:12)
> was His final commandment,
>> the culmination of everything
>>> He ever said and did.

God laid it all out for us through Jesus.

We don't need to guess what God is like.

We have Jesus to tell us.

We don't need to wonder
> what God asks of us or expects from us.

Jesus reveals that to us.

During the process of that revelation,
> through the Sacraments
>> Christ becomes one with us.

Like Him, we too become new Adams and Eves.

We reflect Christ by the good things we say and do.

We become Christ to others
> when we comfort them

        and bring them peace.

Most of all, we reflect Christ
        when we love others as He loves us (See John 13:34).

"Who do people say that *you* are?"

Only you can answer that question.

Do you walk in the footsteps of the Master?

Do you hear His Gospel
        and proclaim that good news
                by the good things you say and do?

        "You are the light of the world . . . your light must shine
        before others so that they may see your good deeds
        and glorify your heavenly Father" (Matt 5:14, 16).

"Who do people say that I am?"

By now we ought to understand the question.

If only we can really understand the answer.

CHAPTER TWO

Acknowledging Our Sins

John the Baptist appeared in the desert proclaiming a baptism for the forgiveness of sins. People of the whole Judean countryside and all the inhabitants of Jerusalem were going out to him and were being baptized by him in the Jordan River as they acknowledged their sins (Mark 1:4-5).

What is sin?

The first century Jews said it was missing the mark,
> "mark" being sort of a moral goal.

God set a standard for Adam and Eve.

> "You are free to eat from any of the trees in the garden except the tree of knowledge of good and bad. From that tree you shall not eat" (Gen 2:16-17).

Christians define sin as not living up to the teachings of Jesus.

Those teachings include the universal commandment
> to love God and neighbor,

> the guidelines found in the Sermon on the Mount

> and the final commandment to love one another
> as Jesus loves us.

For Catholics it was not only failing to live up to the teachings of Jesus but also the laws of the Church.

For example:

> missing Mass on Sunday,
>
> eating meat on days of abstinence,
>
> practicing birth control.

Sin was often defined as an offense against God
> but it could also be an offense against other people.

And, of course, sin has its consequences.

> "From that tree you shall not eat; the moment you eat from it you are doomed to die" (Gen 2:17).

All that said, are sins simply missing the mark,
> disobeying God's laws or Church laws?

It seems to me these definitions fall far short
> of the true meaning of sin.

Sin cannot simply be defined
> as isolated acts against God and neighbor.

Sin must be seen in the context of relationships.

> Aren't we social beings?
>
> Aren't we in relationship with other humans?
>
> Aren't we in relationship with God?

If not we should be!

What about ourselves?

Are we in relationship with ourselves?

Do you talk to yourself?

I bet you do from time to time.

You certainly have many conversations
        with yourself in your thoughts.

For Jesus it was always about relationships.

Read the Sermon on the Mount.

The entire sermon is about relating to God,
        each other and ourselves
                in loving and meaningful ways.

If we don't understand sin
        in terms of harming or hurting relationships
                then we're not only missing the mark;
                      we're missing the point!

How many times do we confess a list of isolated acts?

For many Catholics, it's practically every time they go to confession.

        "I missed Mass on Sunday three times,

        I took God's name in vain twenty times,

        I lied ten times . . ."

We need to throw away the lists
        and think of sin in terms of relationships
                because anything, and I mean anything, we do
                      that hurts or harms our relationship
                            with God, others or with ourselves is sin.

Notice, I didn't say, "a sin".

I said "sin" because sin is rarely, if ever, a single isolated act.

It's a way of life.

When I was a boy, even a young man, I would go to confession weekly
    and I would confess the same sins over and over again.

They rarely, if ever, changed.

Only the numbers changed.

Why didn't they change?

Why didn't the numbers get smaller?

Why was there was no improvement?

I could have made a recording
    and simply played it for the priest!

The problem is
    when we relegate sin to a series of isolated acts
        we rarely put them in the context of relationships.

We objectivize and externalize them.

We were never asked,
    or at least I wasn't, to put our actions in relational terms.

It was cut and dry,
    cold and impersonal.

        And, of course, very private.

We need to think of sin in terms of personal relationships.

We need to think of sin,
    not as an isolated act
        but as a way of life.

Catholics define sin as mortal and venial.

The Church said that venial sins are not serious or grave
    and, therefore the punishment due to that kind of sin
        was not serious or grave.

You could commit millions of venial sins
    and never be afraid of going to hell.

    Maybe thousands of years in purgatory, but not hell!

Mortal sin, however, was different.

Mortal sin, we were told, literally cut us off from God.

There was a total separation, a total loss of grace.

In a sense God turned His back on us,
    as though we never existed.

I bought that as a child
    but no longer as an adult.

The words of St Paul play over in my mind.

> "For I am convinced that neither death, nor life, nor angels, nor principalities, nor present things, nor future things, nor height, nor depth nor any other creature will be able to separate us from the love of God in Christ Jesus our Lord" (Rom 8:38-39).

We certainly can opt to deny God,
    which is to deny love.

We can turn our backs on everything that is good.

But, even if we curse God,
    totally reject God,

> God will still love us;
> > and will still want us to be in Paradise forever.

God will always be there,
> knocking at the door of our hearts,
> > pleading with us to enter there-in.

That said, we can still make a fundamental option against God
> and harden our hearts to love.

That decision is indeed mortal.

Yet, there's a big difference between that
> and missing Mass on Sunday
> > or eating meat on Friday
> > > which the Catholic Church deemed as mortal sins.

Part of the Catholic Church's teaching about sin had to do with its model.

During the course of its history, the Church used several different models.

In the first century the model was Prophetic.

> "First [there are] apostles, second prophets, third teachers . . ." (1 Cor 12:28).

It was a charismatic church
> which was guided by the risen Lord Jesus
> > through the power of the Holy Spirit.

After the Council of Trent, legalism ruled the Church,
> a model similar to the Judaism of the Pharisees.

Law defined sin.

Vatican II moved the Church away from the legal norm into a more personalistic or relational model.

If the Church uses a legal model
> then all of its teaching about sin and damnation is justified.

Law must be defined in terms of degrees
> and punishment must be meted out in terms of the seriousness of the offence.

The problem with a legal model is that it's impersonal.

Every sin and its consequences are clearly spelled out.

It is all black and white.

There is no grey.

The use of conscience as a moral guide plays a minor role.

The Gospels make it clear that Jesus was not a legalist.

In fact, Jesus occasionally broke the laws of Judaism.

> He made mud with His spittle on the Sabbath.

> He told the lame man to pick up his pallet and walk on the Sabbath.

> His disciples picked grain on the Sabbath.

> Jesus ate with sinners.

All these acts were forbidden by Jewish Law.

Paul refused to follow the law of circumcision
> which was passed down by Abraham
>> who received it directly from God!

Based on the Jewish legal model of their time
> both of them sinned and sinned often!

Jesus and Paul were not afraid to question the Law of Moses
        and, at times, they felt they were justified to break it.

They were guided by an informed conscience and,
        a right conscience is always our ultimate moral guide.

They asked the right questions.

        "Can one work on the Sabbath
            if it results in healing a disease or illness?"

        "Can the spirit of the Law supersede the letter of the Law?"

        "Can an informed conscience make judgments contrary to the teachings of Moses?"

The answer is yes to all of the above.

For Jesus, mercy always superseded Jewish Law.

        "I desire mercy, not sacrifice" (Matt 9:13).

The point is morality is not always cut and dry.

        Yes, it will always be wrong to murder,

        to commit adultery,

        to steal and lie.

Those are moral norms that we all intuitively know are wrong.

        "I will place my law within them and write it upon their hearts . . . (Jer 31:33).

However, if you think about those intuitive moral norms
        not a single one of them ever takes place
            outside of the context of human relationships.

If we leave the relationships out then they're just a number.

They're impersonal.

    Confess them.

    Say your penance.

    Pay your debt to society if that's required
        and then get on with your life.

Let me give you an example.

We are all aware of the eighth commandment,

    "You shall not bear false witness against your neighbor".

How many times have you confessed that sin?

I'll bet a lot less than the other nine.

Yet, in today's world,
    it's probably the one commandment
        we break the most and probably never realize it.

The Internet allows people to send messages to whomever about
    political figures, religious leaders, and others.

Most of the senders don't check them out to see if they're true.

Of course, they often only send the ones which support their views
    and most likely don't care if their true
        as long as they get their point across.

I wonder if people realize the damage
    they are doing to a person's reputation
        or how much their messages polarize people.

They probably never think about it
    and I bet they rarely confess it.

That's what happens when sin becomes impersonal.

That's what happens when we don't think of sin
    in terms of how our actions affect our relationships.

And, even when you do confess it, how can you undo the damage?

You can't!

Before Vatican II we called the sacrament penance or confession.

Now, for obvious reasons, we call it reconciliation.

If I hurt or harm a relationship
    then I am obligated
        to restore that relationship to where it was.

I need to, not only confess it,
    but also remedy it.

The big difference here is isolated sins are short term
    but harming relationships are always long term events.

Then we must understand that the actual defined sin
    is only a sign of a sinful life-style.

Think about this.

Can you be a holy, deeply spiritual person
    who has a loving relationship with your husband or
        wife today and commit adultery tomorrow?

    Never!

In order for an adulterous act to occur the relationship had to break down.

>You were already living a sinful lifestyle.

>You were caught up in sinful life patterns.

>Your communication with your spouse broke down.

>If you are a man, you were eyeing other women.

>You probably were lying and uncaring.

Are all those sins?

You bet and worse still,
>taken all together,
>>they make you a sinner
>>>who is living in sin.

Perhaps, if you would have thought of sin in terms of relationships you might have said,

>"My wife and I aren't getting along like we used to."

>"We don't show affection anymore."

>"I'm not as thoughtful as I used to be."

>"We fight a lot."

Then, of course, you have to realize that you need to confess it
>and seek guidance from a priest or minister
>>who might send you to marriage counseling
>>>or convince you to do a Marriage Encounter.

Then too, you might realize the need for prayer,
>even the need for you and your spouse to pray together;
>>whatever it takes to restore your relationship as
>>husband and wife.

If you were to do all that, adultery would never have been an option!

When we think of sin in terms of relationships
      then sin is not simply designated as mortal or venial.

All sin is seen as serious.

Very serious.

> "If your right eye causes you to sin, tear it out and throw it away. It is better for you to lose one of your members than to have your whole body thrown into Gehenna" (Matt 5:29).

This statement by Jesus is hyperbole of course;
      however, nothing must interfere with loving relationships;
           not just with people
                but with God and self.

What happens when we start missing Mass or Sunday services?

Or when we don't pray as much as we used to?

There must be a reason.

Perhaps we doubt the existence of God or that God cares.

Perhaps the real reason is because we're angry with God,
      because we've lost a loved one
           or things aren't working out the way
                we think they should.

Maybe it's none of those.

Maybe we go to Church every Sunday only
      because we feel obligated
           or because we don't want to go to hell.

Maybe the only prayers we pray are the ones
        we learned as a child;
                impersonal and memorized.

Call that a relationship?

        Hardly!

Call that a sinful life pattern?

        Absolutely!

We need to have a "Come to Jesus Meeting" with the Lord
        and anyone else who can help us realize
                that God is a person
                        who desperately wants to be a part of our lives.

We need to realize that we go to church
        because we want to be in the presence of God
                and God's people.

We need to pray from our hearts
        because true and meaningful relationships start there.

Every relationship we have is important
        and perhaps the most important one is with ourselves.

I know it's a cliché, but if we don't really love ourselves
        then we can't love others.

When I say "love ourselves" I mean wanting what's best for us.

To love ourselves begins with self-respect.

        It has nothing to do with narcissism.

        In fact, narcissism is truly a root of evil.

Narcissism is basically and essentially
        what's wrong with the modern world.

We've become so immersed with pleasing ourselves
        that we cannot have true and lasting relationships with others.

We make ourselves into gods
        and spend our lives seeking to only satisfy our own needs.

The fruit of narcissism is hedonism
        in which we feel the most important thing is having fun
                and often without regard for the needs of others.

We end up not only lacking respect for others but also for ourselves.

Self-respect means I realize that I am

        an intellectual,

        physical and

        spiritual being

        who is created in God's image and, as such,
                I must attend to all three of those aspects.
                        because they are what makes me human

That means I can't

        fill my lungs with smoke,

        my body with drugs and alcohol

        or my stomach with too much food,
                especially junk food.

It means I can't fill my mind with trash;

        pornography,

>mindless drivel

>or music that has no melody
>>and is filled with four letter words.

As the old saying goes, "Garbage in, garbage out."

In addition, I have to nurture my soul.

Prayer and private reflection does wonders for the soul.

To leave one's soul unattended is to let it go to waste.

Are all these sins?

What is sin again?

>Anything the hurts or destroys our relationships with people,
>God and ourselves.

We need to constantly examine our relationships
>and ask ourselves questions about
>>how we are nurturing them or harming them.

If we make an honest assessment and ask for help,
>God will provide us with the grace
>>to deal with sin and its consequences.

CHAPTER THREE

Those Who Walk In The Light

Now there was a Pharisee named Nicodemus, a ruler of the Jews. He came to Jesus at night and said to him, Rabbi, we know you are a teacher come from God, for no one can do these signs that you are doing unless God is with him. Jesus answered and said to him, "Amen, amen I say to you, no one can see the kingdom of God without being born from above." Nicodemus said to him, "How can a person, once grown old be born again? Surly he cannot reenter his mother's womb and be born again can he?" Jesus answered, "Amen, amen I say to you, no one can enter the kingdom of God without being born of water and Spirit. What is born of flesh is flesh and what is born of the spirit is spirit" (John 3:1-6).

"Nicodemus came to Jesus at night."

How often do we come to Jesus in darkness?

    The darkness of ignorance.

    The darkness of our sinfulness.

    The darkness of doubt.

    The darkness of despair.

It seems like we seek Him more often in our dark hours
    than times when everything is going well for us.

When we are doing well,

    when we are healthy and have a good job,

> when our kids are excelling in school,
>
> when our marriage is stable,
>
> when we have enough money to pay our bills,

we rarely seek Jesus.

But, when life is a downer,

> when we're sad or depressed,
>
> when we are ill or our relationships are strained,
>
> when we've lost the way,

that's when we look to Jesus for help.

We come to Him in the darkness
> of our troubled hearts and empty souls.

Some of us don't even do it even then
> but, thank God, most do.

I say, "Thank God"
> because Jesus is the light
> > that comes into our darkness.

> > "The light shines in the darkness and the darkness has not overcome it" (John 1:5).

It's amazing how we often prefer to grope in the darkness,
> thinking and believing that we can find the way.

Yet, without the light of Christ
> we can never find the way.

> > "I am the way . . ." (John 14:6).

Too often we put our trust in people.

Jeremiah said,

> "Cursed is the one who puts his trust in men" (Jer 17:5).

Have you ever known a perfect human being?

> One who would never let you down?

> Whose feet weren't made of clay?

> Who never sinned or hurt another person?

Yet, we commit ourselves to politicians
> who rarely live up to their promises,
>> who use their power for personal gain:
>>> men and women whose personal lives are a shambles.

It doesn't make any difference
> whether they're Republicans or Democrats.

They say whatever needs to be said to get elected
> but they rarely, if ever, deliver.

Why do we rely on priests and ministers
> who abuse our children,
>> steal money from the collections,
>>> and consort with prostitutes and drug dealers?

We make athletes and movie stars into idols
> wishing we were like them.

Yet, some of them are among
> the most despicable people on this planet.

They are narcissistic and self-centered,
> waste enormous amounts of money on self-indulgence
> and more often than not their lives are a terrible

        example for our children.

What are we thinking?

Where are our priorities?

These people are liars, cheaters, adulterers
        and God only knows what else.

Jeremiah was right.

He understood how weak we really are.

So why not put your faith in Jesus?

He was the perfect man,
        the one in whom you can put all your trust.

He is the God-man
        who will lead you out of the darkness of evil
            into the light of God's grace.

He is the one who offers us re-birth-
        to be "born again from above".

Those who walk in the light are indeed reborn.

They, like everyone else, are born into the family of mankind,
        but through baptism are reborn into the family of God.

How often do you think of yourself as God's own son or daughter?

If not, then you should!

We are all God's children.

Know that you are a child of God.

That makes you special.

Very special.

There has never been another human being exactly like you.

You are one of a kind!

But it also makes you accountable.

For, if we are God's children
> then we must behave like God's children.

We must be children of the light.

Jesus, who is the light,
> will lead you out of the darkness
>> into the light of His truth.

It's his truth that will set you free
> because, in its light, there is nothing hidden.

There are no masks to hide behind.

We don't need to pretend.

We can freely be the person God wants us to be,
> the person we are meant to be.

The light of Christ will reveal our innermost selves.

The light of Christ will transform us from flesh and blood,
> which will die, into an eternal spirit
>> which will live forever with God.

Can it ever be better than that?

What does it matter if you live a hundred years

or even five hundred years?

If you remain in the flesh you will always end up as dust!

But in the spirit you will live forever
        because your spirit will be joined to God's Spirit
                and God's Spirit is eternal.

Why don't we want that?

Why can't we seem to get it?

How long must we see our friends and loved ones die
        before we understand that in the flesh,
                life's a dead end.

"If Jesus did not rise then we are the most pitiable of men" (1 Cor 15).

But if our flesh houses a spirit,
        which is from God,
                united to God,
                      then there is cause to rejoice.

"Rejoice and be glad for your reward will be great in heaven" (Matt 5:12).

All of us were born into the family of mankind.

Now we need to be reborn into the family of God-

        born from above.

Members of the family of God are different.

We don't lord it over others; we serve others,
        even when they are undeserving of our service.

We don't seek to be first;
        we seek to be last

    so others can be first.

We don't love so we can be loved in return.

We love so that others can know what it's like to be loved.

Members of the family of God imitate Christ.

He gave His life
    so that others could live.

    "No one has greater love than this, to lay down one's life for one's friends" (John 15:13).

Perhaps we will never be called to do this
    but we must be willing to do it and,
        if we are truly reborn from above,
            we will gladly do it!

Christ is our perfect model.

There has never been anyone like Him
    nor will there ever be anyone like Him.

Nicodemus knew He was different.

    "Rabbi, we know you are a teacher who has come from God . . ." (John 3:2).

Not only has He come from God;
    He is the revelation of God!

    "My teaching is not my own but from the one who sent me" (John 7:16).

If Jesus is the revelation of God
    then the way to understand God is to listen to Jesus.

Jesus is always revealing God to us,
>   first and foremost in the Gospels
>   >   but also in the liturgy,
>   >   >   through the teaching body of the Church
>   >   >   >   and, believe it or not, in the person next to you.

These are ways we come to know the Father.

We need to remember that the Holy Spirit is everywhere
>   and, when we allow ourselves to be

>   embraced by the Spirit,

>   inspired by the Spirit,

>   moved by the Spirit,

then we are touched by the ever-present Spirit of Christ
>   who is our brother.

Yes, our brother.

Since we are born from above
>   we are a brother or a sister of the one who came from above.

>   ". . . the word who was with God . . . became flesh"
>   (John 1:1, 14).

To be born from above means we need to let go of everything
>   that ties us to the ways of the world.

That doesn't mean we despise the world or become hermits.

For some, that may be the case but for most it's not.

We live in the world, we are part of the world
>   but we do not belong to the world;
>   >   we belong to God.

"... you do not belong to the world because I have
chosen you out of the world" (John 15:19).

Since we belong to God
    we must live as God wants us to live.

    We must live in the Spirit.

That means,
    while we can't be separated from the world,
        we must not be attached to the things of the world.

What is more important, your spouse or your car?

What means more to you, your children or your bank account?

Too many people put their jobs ahead of their family.

Jobs are important.

We need a place to live and money in the bank to survive
    but when the time comes for us to leave this earth,
      few, if any, ever say,

    "I wish I had earned more money or my
    house wasn't big enough."

People don't worry about those things when they're dying.

"Nicodemus came to Jesus at night . . ."

To live in a world
    where things replace people
        and where activities replace relationships
           is to live in darkness.

Since we have been baptized,
    born from above,

        we walk in the light.

    There is no darkness.

Not even the shadow of death
      can quench the light,
           which has been given to us.

Only the shadow of sin can do that.

For those born from above there is no death; only life and light.

CHAPTER FOUR

God Does Not Cause Suffering

As he passed by he saw a man blind from birth. His disciples asked him, "Rabbi, who sinned, this man or his parents, that he was born blind? Jesus answered, "Neither he nor his parents sinned; it is so that the works of God might be made visible through him. (John 9:1-3)

What a strange question?

Why on earth would the disciples believe
    that God would visit blindness on a man because of his sins?

        Especially, since he was born blind.

How could he possibly have any personal sin before he was born?

And then, what do his parents' sins have to do with his blindness?

One wonders what kind of God these people believed in.

Actually, since most didn't believe in an afterlife,
    they believed God rewarded and punished them in this life.

And, if not in this life,
    it would be meted out to one's progeny.

    After all, God is just, right?

Jesus tells us that suffering in this life
    has little or nothing to do with punishment from God.

Suffering as a punishment from God is the way of the Old Covenant.

Jesus has ushered in the new and everlasting covenant.

In this covenant, death doesn't end in dust;

> it opens the door to eternal life.

Let me ask you:

> What kind of god would cause a person to be blind?
>
> What kind of god would cause cancer or heart disease or aids?
>
> Why would you worship such a god?

Jesus makes it very clear.

> God does not cause blindness or any other malady.

If that were the case then why did Jesus heal people?

God sent Jesus to alleviate suffering not cause it.

Yet so many people say, "Oh, it was God's will that he suffered."

> "It was God's will to take him."
>
> "It was his time."

These people are fatalists
who have a very different image of the God Jesus loves.

> The God of Jesus lets it rain on the just as well as the unjust (Matt 5:45).
>
> The God of Jesus welcomes the sinner with open arms (Lk 15:20).

    The God of Jesus promises paradise to criminals (Lk 23:42).

That's the God we are called to believe in.

That's the God we are called to worship.

Don't mix God up with the gods of wood and stone,
    the gods of the superstitious and the ignorant.

Our God is different.

    Our God heals us.

    Our God lifts us up.

    Our God forgives us and calls us to everlasting life where
    ". . . there will be no more death or mourning, wailing or pain"
    (Rev 21:4).

"But we suffer," you say.

Even Jesus suffered,
    and more so than most.

He was crucified, hung from a cross to die alone in shame.

All the more reason to believe
    that God doesn't punish us in this life with suffering and death
    because of our sins.

    Jesus was not a sinner.

    In fact, He never sinned.

Still He suffered. Why?

Many believe that God sent His son
    to suffer and die on the cross.

How can they believe that?

Would you commit your son to death,
        death on the cross?
        I'm sure you wouldn't.

Are you more merciful than God?

        Hardly!

So how can you say that God would
        condemn His beloved to death-
                a terrible death at that?

God would never send His son to suffer and die on the cross.

God sent Jesus to reveal God to us
        and to redeem us from our sins.

Evil men plotted against Him and had Him crucified.

"But," you ask,

        "If God is so good then why would God let them kill His son?"

Why does God allow war, cancers, genocide, earthquakes, and hurricanes?

I'm not sure I know the answer to that question,
        but, unlike some seem to believe,
                it's not because so many people have sinned
                        that God had to teach them a lesson.

Think about this a moment.

Jesus suffered and died on the Cross.

He became a curse.

        "Cursed rests on him who is hung from a tree" (Deut 21:23).

We killed our God!

No one made us kill Him.

We did it freely!

Well, you and I didn't literally kill Him.

Evil men did 2000 years ago,
>	but we belong to the family of mankind
>>		and just as we share guilt in the sin of Adam
>>>			so we share guilt in the death of Christ.

In the name of justice,
>	God had every right to destroy this earth.

In the name of justice,
>	God should have sent famines and plagues
>>		to pay us back for what we had done.

But God didn't choose to do that because it's not justice God seeks.

>	It's mercy (Matt 12:7).

So, instead of condemning us and punishing us,
>	God chose to turn that
>>		bleak, dark, terrible Friday into a Good Friday.

Jesus' death became the ultimate sacrifice,
>	an offering for the sins of mankind.

Can you imagine that?

We kill God's beloved Son, pound nails into Him, hang Him from a tree
>	and, instead of getting even,
>>		God chose to use that atrocity to redeem us.

God took the curse

   and transformed Him into a Savior.

How can you believe that a God who does that
   causes suffering and disasters
     that kills and maims thousands of people?

So why do we suffer?

Parts of that answer lies with us.

How much suffering do we cause?

How many wars have the people of the human race started?

Why, we've even dared to start them in the name of God!

Such things are indeed the consequences of sin.

  We lie,

  cheat,

  steal,

  commit adultery,

  murder,

  destroy other people's property

and then wonder why the world is so messed up.

Then some have the audacity to blame the woes of the world on God!

Talk about passing the buck!

The primary cause of suffering in this world is us.
We are selfish creatures

> who may have been created in the image and likeness of God
> but we sure don't act like it.

God certainly isn't like us

If He were we'd be in deep trouble!

Our problem is that we fashion God into our image
> and sometimes we make God into our worst selves.

Too many of us can't even begin to imagine how good God is;
> how much God loves us
> > and desires to reward us with the everlasting joys of heaven.

> ". . . eye has not seen, ear has not heard nor has it entered the human heart what God has prepared for those who love him . . ." (1 Cor 2:9)

God wants you to go to heaven far more that you do.

Can you believe God is that good?

Sadly many can't.

For them God is the Old Testament's

> ". . . jealous God who inflicts punishment for their father's wickedness on the children of those who hate me down to the third and fourth generation . . ." (Ex 20:5).

What does the Letter to the Hebrews say?

> "In times past, God spoke in partial and various ways to our ancestors through the prophets; in these last days he spoke to us through his son . . ." (Heb 1:1).

The key word here is "partial".

The revelation of God in the Old Testament is incomplete.

Pieces of the puzzle are missing.

But now we have the full revelation of God
    that's been given to us through His Son,
        Jesus who is the Word of God.

There are no longer any pieces missing.

Everything we need to know for our salvation has been revealed to us.

What does the first letter of John say?

    "God is love . . ." (1 Jn 4:8)

He doesn't say, "God loves" or, "God is loving".

God and love are the same.

In New Testament Greek the word is *agape*,
which means divine love.

Divine love is a love that always wants what's best for the beloved.

    "You are God's chosen ones, holy and beloved" (Col 3:12).

If God always wants what's best for you
    is He going to make you suffer and die?

I hardly think so.

God gives life,

    "life that was the light of the human race" (Jn 1:3).

God turned Good Friday into Easter Sunday.

That's why we call it *Good* Friday.

At the time, there was nothing "good" about it.

Just ask Jesus.

Ask His disciples.

It was the blackest Friday ever
>but now,
>>because of the goodness of God,
>>>it's our greatest blessing.

If God can turn that Good Friday into an Easter Sunday
>don't you think God can turn your darkest, most nightmarish days into Easter Sundays?

I would certainly hope so.

You are God's beloved!

Sometimes we don't recognize those Easter Sundays
>because God doesn't answer our prayers
>>the way we want Him to.

We ask questions like,

>"Why did I have to get sick?"

>"How come God doesn't cure my cancer?"

>"Why did my husband die of a heart attack?

>"How could God let me lose my job?"

Why do we believe God did it?

Did you ever stop to think how many people are diagnosed with cancer every day?

      Or how many die of heart attacks.

Your case is one of many; thousands; tens of thousands!

So, if God's responsible for you or your loved one's misfortune
      then God's responsible for everyone's misfortune.

That means that God is one big troublemaker!

Now, don't believe that because you're a good person
      you're not going to suffer.

Read the lives of the saints. See how many of them suffered.

Jesus was the most perfect human being and yet,
      He suffered, suffered death by crucifixion.

It can't get any worse than that!

Suffering, disease and death are an integral part of what it means to be human.

      Dying is a part of living.

      It's just the way it is.

      Deal with it!

The problem is that we see
      only a very small part of the picture,
            and inkling of the master plan-

            God's plan.

God sees it all
> and God has the power to put it all into place.

God truly has the power to turn our dark and terrible Fridays into Easter Sundays.

He wouldn't be God if He couldn't do that.

Trust in God.

Believe that God wants what's best for you.

Know that God loves you and calls you to be a part of His plan
> because

>> ". . . all things work for the good of those who love God, who are called according to his purpose" (Rom 8:28).

Believe that God is good, only does what is good
> and always wants what's best for you
>> and for the whole world.

"Why was this man born blind?"

It was not God's doing.

God's doing was to make him see.

Hopefully, we can see too!

CHAPTER FIVE

Lord, Teach Us To Pray

Jesus was praying in a certain place and when he had finished, one of his disciples said to him, "Lord, teach us to pray just as John taught his disciples." He said to them, "When you pray say: Father, hallowed be your name, your kingdom come. Give us each day our daily bread and forgive us our sins as we ourselves forgive everyone in debt to us and do not subject us to the final test" (Lk 11:1-4).

It amazes me that the disciples asked Jesus how to pray.

They were devout Jews.

They prayed at least three times a day:

> "Hear O Israel, the Lord is our God. Therefore you shall love the Lord your God with all your heart, and with all your soul and with all your strength" (Deut 6:5).

So begins the Schema,
    the sacred prayer of the Jews
        given to them in the book of Deuteronomy.

It was the prayer they were commanded to teach their children,
    a prayer they were to write on their wrists
        and on the doorposts of their houses.

Later, they would add the well-known phrase,

> "You shall love your neighbor as you love yourself."

The Jews were people of prayer.

They prayed morning, noon and night.

On feast days and the Sabbath
    they devoted the entire day to prayer.

Certainly, they knew how to pray.

Yet, the disciples, all Jews, ask Jesus to teach them to pray.

Was there something special about the way Jesus prayed?

    There must have been
        and when they saw it they felt inadequate
           or so spiritually impoverished
                they knew they needed help.

What made His prayers so different?

    Simplicity was part of it.

Notice His response.

Luke's version of the Lord's Prayer
    is much shorter than Matthew's;
        only 38 words versus 52.

    Still, both are very short.

What does Jesus say in Matthew 6:7?

    "In praying, don't babble like the pagans, who think they will be heard because of their many words."

How often do we pray the same prayers over and over again?

They become so ingrained in our minds, they're mindless.

We don't even pay attention to what we are saying anymore.

Yet, we think that the more we repeat them
        the more likely God will hear them
                and maybe answer them.

But Jesus says in Matt 6:8,

        "Your Father knows what you want *before* you ask
        him" (italics mine).

So why do you keep repeating the same prayers over and over again?

Is it because you think you can wear God down?

Or maybe it's because
        God might forget what it is that you want!

After all God's quite old!

Who knows what's best for you, you or God?

I doubt any of you said you know better.

So then why do you feel
        you have to keep telling God what you want?

Most of our prayers are what
        I call the "gimme-do-me" prayers.

They are basically prayers
        which tell God what we want or need.

It's the prayer that says I know what's best for me
        and now I need to convince God that I am right!

What does Matthew's Our Father say?

> "Your will be done" (Matt 6:10).

What did Jesus say in the Garden of Gethsemane?

> "Not what I will, but what you will" (Mark 14:36).

What did Mary say to the angel Gabriel?

> "May it be done to me according to your word"(Lk 1:38).

I think one of the things about Jesus
> that impressed His disciples
>> to the point of asking Him how to pray
>>> was His total dependence on the will of His Father.

Jesus doesn't seem to ask for much.

> "My food is to do the will of him who sent me"(John 4:34).

But instead of doing God's will
> we're always asking God for something aren't we?

And so often, in our asking,
> we babble on like the pagans do!

In fact, most of us pray like pagans!

So many of us think that if we say the right words,

> if we say them the right number of times,

> if we genuflect enough

> or bow our heads properly

  or say particular prayers for an exact number of days
  our wishes will be granted.

That's exactly what pagan prayer is.

Pagan prayer is designed to appease the gods,
  make them change their minds,
    cajole them enough so
      they will give us what we want.

Pagan prayer is entirely based on the desire to change God;
  to alter His disposition in our favor.

The pagans envisioned their gods as being like them;
  in fact the Mesopotamian gods were deemed worse than humans.

They were angry and capricious despots
  who needed to be highly pleased
    before they answered any petitions,
      if they answered them at all.

Most of them were seen as trying to make humans miserable.

So mortals sacrificed animals to feed their gods with burnt flesh
  or they offered incense to please them with soothing odors.

One might call that ancient aroma therapy!

And if one type of prayer or action didn't work
  they'd try another or many others,
    even to the point of sacrificing humans
      in order to get their petitions answered.

Why is it so difficult for us
  to let go of what we've decided is good for us
    and let God do what God has wanted to do in us
      since the day we were born?

"Thy will be done on earth as it is in heaven."

If God knows what's best for you
    then why would you ask for anything
        except that God's will be done in and through you?

I know you've heard this before:
    it is not we who change God,
        it's God who changes us.

To believe that we can change God
    is to try to bring God down to our level.

That's why it's pagan.

We're fashioning God into our image
    not the other way around.

That's not the real purpose of prayer

Prayer is not for God's benefit.

It's for our benefit.

Quite frankly, God doesn't need our prayers.

God is not petty and small like us.

God doesn't have an ego problem.

He's not narcissistic.

God doesn't need us to tell Him
    how wonderful He is,
        how perfect,
           powerful
                or great He is.

We need to truly believe that
        so we can finally realize how weak and impotent
                we are without God.

We need to realize that without God
        we are heading down a dead-end street,
            a road to nowhere.

So prayer is for us not God.

It is our holy longing for the divine presence in our lives.

It is our deepest yearning to get in touch
        with the Spirit of God
            who dwells in us.

        "Do you not know that your body is a temple of the
        Holy Spirit" (1 Cor 6:19)?

So, why do we pray?

We pray in order to encounter God
        and to become open enough to understand
            what God expects from us.

We pray so that we can truly become
        what we are meant to be-
            the image of God.

Doing that requires faith.

A lot of people don't pray
        because they have no faith.

If you don't believe in God
        or you don't believe God cares about you
            then why pray?

It would be like talking to the wall
    or talking to yourself.

"But," you ask, "how would you know
    that the whole exercise isn't an illusion?"

The truth is you don't know for sure
    but you *believe* that it is real,
    and once you truly encounter God in the deepest
    recesses of your heart
        you know that God is real
            and that your experience of God is real.

It's when you feel the imprint of God's hands
    molding and shaping you into the image of Love.

Someone once said,

    "It is not you who shape God; it is God who shapes you."

    If this is true, you must remain soft and pliable
        so that you can feel the imprint of His fingers.

God fashioned Adam in this way
    and when he allowed the Divine Potter to shape him thusly,
        God became his companion.

God walked with him in the garden,
    talked to him every day and,
        he felt the breath of God in every fiber of his being.

We need to be like Adam,
    not the Adam who failed
        but, as Paul says, the new Adam who is Jesus.
        (See Rom 5:12-21)

    And, we need to pray like Him.

So then, how did he pray?

Jesus cried out "*Abba*" the Aramaic word for "daddy'!

Paul says,

> ". . . you have received the spirit of adoption through which we cry out *Abba* . . ." (Rom 8:15).

"Daddy" is too familiar for us
> so we translate it using the more formal "Father".

How could we dare to call God "dad"?

Jesus didn't seem to have a problem
> and He literally tells us to call God "daddy"!

> "Our *daddy* which art in Heaven."

> "*Daddy*, take this cup away from me . . ."

It seems strange to address God that way doesn't it?

It's seems almost sacrilegious.

That's our problem. "God's up in Heaven," we say,
> "and we're down here".

And God is up there because,
> well, because He's God.

He's the Almighty.

We're supposed to fear Him aren't we?"

Are we?

If you have a really good relationship with your father
> is it because you're afraid of him?

Respect, yes; afraid, no.

That's what Jesus is trying to teach His disciples and us.

God is our heavenly dad
>   who always wants what's best for us
>   >   and, most importantly, knows what's best for us.

"But", you say, "if God knows what's best for us
>   why do we suffer and why do we die?"

As I said in the previous chapter, God sees the whole picture.

We only see a very small part of it.

In fact it's such a very small part
>   we could never even begin to understand the plan.

>   "My thoughts are not your thoughts, nor are my ways your ways, says the Lord" (Isaiah 55:8).

What we need to do
>   is see ourselves as adult children of God, whom
>   >   we can never fully understand but,
>   >   >   whom we can relate to in a mature way.

Let's go back to the creation of Adam.

The story in Genesis 2 describes Adam as a child of God
>   but he's not an infant;

>   he's an adult child
>   >   and he is treated as an adult—with love and respect.

God gives first man and first woman adult responsibilities.

>   "Have dominion over the fish of the sea . . . and all the living things that move on the earth" (Gen 1:28).

WORDS TO LIVE BY

We have to understand

> we are no longer little children.
>
> We are adults and our faith must be that of an adult.
>
> "When I was a child, I used to talk as a child, think as a child, reason as a child; when I became a man, I put aside my childish ways" (1 Cor 13:11).

When it comes to prayer we need to put aside our childish ways.

Adults don't keep asking their parents for things.

Or at least they shouldn't!

They no longer need someone to change their diapers,
> kiss their booboos, or feed them.

When we grow up our parents become our friends, our confidants.

We are still their child
> but we are no longer treated like a child.

In a sense, we become friends.

Jesus told His disciples,

> "I no longer call you slaves because a slave does not know what his master is doing. Instead I have called you friends . . ." (John 15:15).

One becomes an adult
> when he or she no longer expects material things from his or her parents.

They can take care of themselves;
> they only need to give love and receive love in return.

So it's the same with God.

When we see God as our divine parent,
        as adult believers we no longer hanker for gifts
                or ask for the things
                        that we ourselves can take care of.

God is not man's alibi,
        nor an excuse for not being human.

We need to understand
        that God has already given us everything we need for salvation.

        "God . . . has blessed us in Christ with every spiritual gift
in the heavens . . ." (Eph 1:3).

So we don't need to ask God for anything.

We need to thank God and praise God
        for all the wonderful gifts He's given us!

The Liturgy of the Hours is the prayer of the Church. It used to be called the Breviary and is based on the Psalms.

Priests and Deacons pray these prayers every day.

Morning and Evening Prayer ends with a list of petitions.

Some examples of these petitions are:

        "God of mercy hear the prayers we offer for all your people . . ."

        "Look with love on all who are to be reborn in baptism . . ."

        "Open the door to eternal happiness to all the dead . . ."

These prayers often end with words like,

>"Be merciful to us Lord," or

>"Help us with your grace."

These are beautiful prayers
>and I'm sure God is pleased with the one who wrote them,
>>however, they ask God to do things He's already done!

They imply that perhaps God needs to be persuaded to answer them.

Wouldn't it be better to say:

>"You are a merciful God who always hears the prayers of your people . . ."

>"Loving Father, you look lovingly on all those reborn in baptism . . ."

>"Lord, you open the door to eternal happiness to all the dead."

A more proper response to this type of prayer might be,

>"Thank you Lord" or

>"Praise you Father."

Praying in this way re-affirms what is true;
>what God is already doing for us and in us.

Do you think for one second that the "Abba" of Jesus
>would never listen to our prayers
>>or not look with love on us
>>>or ever close the door to eternal life?

We need to do an exchange.

We need to exchange the "gimme-do-me" for praise and thanksgiving.

What follows *Our Father*?

"*Hallowed* be thy name" (italics mine).

Hallowed means *holy*
        and what is holy should be honored.

How do we honor God?

We praise Him!

Jesus' prayers are always about praise and thanksgiving.

> "Father (Abba), the hour has come. Give glory to your son so that your son may glorify (praise) you" (John 17:1).

> "Father (Abba) I thank you for hearing me" (John 12:41).

St Paul learned how to pray as Jesus prayed.

> "Praised be the God and Father of our Lord Jesus Christ . . . (Eph 1:3).

> "I always give thanks to my God . . ." (1 Cor 1:4).

> "First I give thanks to my God through Jesus Christ for all of you . . ." (Rom 1:8).

These are but a few of the scores of examples of praise
        and thanksgiving found on the lips of Jesus
                and those who believed in Him.

Read Psalm 150.

Almost every single line begins with the word "Praise".

So, do you want to pray as Jesus prayed?
>   As He taught His followers to pray?

Then throw away those gimme-do-me requests
>   and replace them with praise and thanksgiving!

So am I saying you should thank God
>   when you're sick or when something terrible happens?

Yes you should, if you want to pray as an adult.

> "I am troubled now. Yet, what should I say? Father, save me from this hour. It was for this purpose that I came to this hour" (John 12:27).

Jesus understood that God knew what was best
>   even though, sometimes, it made no sense to Him.

We need to learn to do the same.

I love the prayer of St Ignatius Loyola,

> "Take Lord, receive all I have and possess. You have given all to me, now I return it. Give me only your love and your grace. That's enough for me."

Shouldn't God's love and grace always be enough
>   no matter where we are in life?

>   What can be better than that?

When we get to the point
>   where we understand
>>   that God's shares his life with us (the meaning of the word grace)
>>>   and that God truly loves us far more than we can ever imagine,
>>>>   then we will stop acting like children
>>>>>   and start praying like adults.

ROBERT TREMMEL

"Lord, will you teach us how to pray?"

That's the question.

Perhaps now you have the answer.

CHAPTER SIX

Forgiveness Leads To Love

Then Jesus turned to the woman and said to Simon. "Do you see this woman? When I entered your house, you did not give me water for my feet, but she has bathed them with her tears and wiped them with her hair. You did not give me a kiss, but she has not ceased kissing my feet since the time I entered. You did not anoint my head with oil, but she has anointed my feet with ointment. So I tell you, her many sins have been forgiven; hence she has shown great love. But the one to whom little is forgiven, loves little" (Luke 7:43-47).

Forgiveness leads to love.

How often have you considered that axiom?

Unless you've read the above reading carefully,
        perhaps never.

Those who feel neither God nor others have forgiven them
        become hard hearted.

They are like a stone.

The tenderness they felt as a child is gone.

Yet, it is as important to forgive
        as it is to be forgiven.

When we refuse to forgive
        we not only steal away the transgressor's peace and joy
               but our own as well.

Love is stolen from the offender
    and the one offended.

And what did Jesus say?

    "Love one another as I have loved you" (John 15:12).

Jesus had an inexhaustible ability to love
    because He, as the God-man,
        had and has the unlimited capacity to forgive.

Part of His ability to forgive was because He was so humble.

The reason there is so little love in the world
    is because there is so much self-righteousness.

The proud and the arrogant rule the world.

It seems like everyone's forgotten, "Blessed are the meek."

There are so many people who,
    not only believe they're right,
        but also <u>know</u> they're right.

There are so many who try to oppress
    and control others with their absolute knowledge.

They know and have the truth.

At least they think they do.

So many people have never felt the healing balm of forgiveness,
    and, it's often because they never were able to forgive.

They never said the words. "I forgive you."

Most likely, they rarely, if ever, have said "I'm sorry."

That's because they know it all and,
    at least in their minds, never make a mistake.

Those who feel they have the absolute truth
    leave little room for fellowship
        and certainly no room for dialogue.

How sad.

Can't we ever understand
    that only God has the absolute truth
        and because we are not God we'll never have it.

We only brush up against it once in a while.

    "We walk by faith and not by sight" (2 Cor 5:7).

I wonder.

    Does it ever occur to them that they might be wrong?

I don't know about you
    but as I get older I seem to find
        I'm wrong at least 50% of the time.

When I thought I was right
    I offended far more people than I did
        when I kept my mouth shut!

Can you imagine how different the world would be
    if people were truly humble;

    if they would admit that there are others
        who are more important than they;

    if they could allow themselves to be less
    so that someone else could be more?

Can you imagine what kind of world
    there would be if
        people could readily admit their guilt
           and say they're sorry
                instead of making excuses
                    to cover up their offences?

Can you image what kind of world there would be
    if we truly understood
        that love is not so much about passion and feelings
            as it is about wanting what's best for others
                even if we don't like them?

Forgiveness opens up all these opportunities.

Think of all the people we could set free
    if we were more forgiving.

    Not just others but ourselves as well.

I know so many people who refuse to let it go.

They hang on to all the hatred and the need for revenge.

They can't forget
    and so they can't forgive.

Who are they hurting the most?

The answer is simple
    and most of us know it.

Yet, the truth is we hurt both ourselves
    and the one we refuse forgiveness.

Give it up!

The past is the past. It's over.

It can only be replayed in your mind
> and only if you want to.

It will never happen again.

Life goes on
> and will continue to go on in spite of your hard-heartedness.

Why not take the chance
> and offer your forgiveness.

Think of the healing that can take place.

Think of the love you can instill!

"But", you say,

> "I can't find it within myself to forgive."

> "I was terribly hurt."

> "The wound is still there."

Then you must pray for the grace to forgive.

> "Grace and mercy are with his holy ones" (Wis 3:9).

Often, we need God's grace to empower us to forgive.

The old saying, "To err is human, to forgive is divine" is very true.

I can never understand
> why we continue to try to do things without God.

It must be our egos or a lack of humility.

Perhaps, when we were young we were told,
> "God helps those who help themselves".

That's true but that doesn't mean we leave God out!

We are called to be in a partnership with God.

That's the way it originally was in the Garden of Eden
        and it's still that way today.

As God walked in the garden with Adam
        He can walk in this world with you.

Ask Him to be your companion on your journey of life.

He will never refuse you.

How often have you prayed for the grace to forgive?

I bet, for some, never!

If your answer is never
        then you better start now
               because you will never enter the Kingdom of Heaven.

        "For, if you do not forgive others their transgressions,
        neither will your heavenly Father forgive you" (Matt 6:15).

"Still," some of you say, "I've prayed for a forgiving heart
        but in this case, I cannot forgive this person."

Then pray for God's forgiveness.

Partner with God
        and allow God's forgiveness to flow through you.

To forgive really is divine
        and sometimes we need to allow God to use us
                to bring forgiveness to the one
                        who desperately needs it.

We can be conduits of God grace, God's forgiveness and God's love.

In the opening scripture for this chapter,
    we hear Jesus tell Simon a lot more
        about this woman's heart and soul
            than anyone seems to know.

She was obviously a hard core sinner.

The Pharisee knew it.

Most likely everyone in the town knew it.

She had a reputation.

Who was this woman?

Let's suppose, just for the sake of making a point,
    she was the woman caught in adultery,
        the story found in John 8:3-11.

Actually, she might have been
    since the story is not found in the earliest Johanine manuscripts.

In fact, the style and language is more like Luke than John.

In that scene, she was on the verge of being stoned to death.

She was thrown on the ground
    and shamefully lay there shaking and weeping,
        anxiously waiting for the first stone to open her skull.

But the stone never came.

Instead, she heard Jesus say,

    "Let the one among you who is without sin be the first

to throw a stone at her" (8:9).

Ironically, they all leave.

Soon she's alone with Jesus.

She is unharmed
> but there's still an ache in her soul
> > and a pain in her heart.

She knows she's a sinner and deserves to be punished.

After all, that's God's way isn't it?

But the God of Jesus replaces justice with mercy
> and so she hears the words she has longed to hear.

> > "Neither do I condemn you. Go and from now on do not sin any more" (John 8:11).

Can you imagine how she must have felt?

Perhaps, for the first time in her life she knows
> what it means to be loved.

And now she knows what it means to be forgiven.

Never again will she seek out a sordid affair.

Never again will she use her body to find love.

From that moment on she is determined to love others
> as she has been loved.

"So I tell you, her many sins have been forgiven;
> hence she has shown great love."

Her encounter with Jesus opened the doorway to grace.

Jesus had wiped away the past.

Someone was able to look beyond the external filth
        and saw the image of God residing within her.

He saw her true beauty.

All the sin in the world
        couldn't hide that from Jesus!

How different Jesus is from us.

More often than not we never look past the surface.

We pride ourselves for finding fault in others.

We're so quick to judge, so quick to condemn.

After all, if we highlight another's sins
        we can redirect attention away from our own sinfulness.

Then we can keep up the pretense
        that we are holy and good.

Yet, when we do that
        we place ourselves in the company of the self-righteous
        Pharisees.

And what did Jesus have to say about them?

        "Woe to you, scribes and Pharisees, you hypocrites.
        You are like white-washed tombs, which appear beautiful
        on the outside, but inside you are filled with dead men's
        bones and every kind of filth" (Matt 23:27).

The Pharisees were the holiest men in all of Israel.

They were good and decent people
    who went far beyond the Law of Moses.

But they were heartless.

They stoned women to death.

They cursed the lepers, the blind and the lame,
    calling them sinners, telling them they had no hope.

Sound familiar?

The world is still full of Pharisees
    and many of them call themselves Christians!

So, whether or not we are Pharisees
    why are most of us so reluctant to call ourselves sinners?

Part of the answer is that we don't want to change
    and we certainly don't want God to change us.

So many people are afraid of change.

Look what happened after Vatican II.

Some people are still trying to go back to
    "the way it used to be" or
        "the way it always was".

If you think the Church never changed,
    you've never read its history.

Change is God's way.

It must be God's way because everything changes.

Nothing in the universe stays the same.

It is endlessly expanding.

The law of the conservation of matter says
        "nothing can be created or destroyed,
              it can only be changed."

In fact, it is always changing.

We need to change as well
        and as a matter of fact,
              whether we want to or not
                      we *are* changing.

Change is good for us.

Another reason we refuse to admit our sinfulness
        has to do with ego.

We're too proud to admit that we're flawed.

We are so conscious of appearances
        and so concerned about what people think of us
              that we lie to ourselves and others to appear virtuous.

Look at all the ways we cover up our sins with our jargon.

We no longer lie,
        we just juggle the facts a bit or stretch the truth.

People no longer commit adultery,
        they fool around or,
               as they say, "hook up".

We don't cheat,
        we just pad our expense accounts
              or fudge the numbers a bit.

It's not "pro-abortion"
> it's "pro-choice".

One doesn't kill the fetus;
> he simply extracts it.

The truth is we are what we are
> and no amount of clever verbiage
> > can hide or change that.

We are sinners and we need to admit it.

There are no valid cover-ups when it comes to sin.

> "If we say we are without sin, we deceive ourselves and the truth is not in us . . . If we say 'we have not sinned' we make God a liar, and his word is not in us" (1 John 1:8,10).

To commit sin is not the worst evil.

It's to commit sin and deny it.

Everyone is a sinner;
> everyone is flawed,
> > even the Dali Lama and the Pope!

Read the lives of the Popes some day
> and you'll find out how many were far more sinful
> > than the woman caught in adultery!

So fess up.

We are all sinners in need of redemption.

Say it!

We need to understand that Jesus didn't come to abolish sin.

He came to forgive it in the hope that,
    once forgiven, we'd learn to love!

Many don't believe that they *can* be forgiven.

That's because they've never encountered the love of Christ.

The love of Christ has no obstacles.

There are few, if any conditions; no boundaries,
    no circumstances which need to be addressed.

The only condition Jesus placed on the woman caught in adultery
    was that she avoid sin,
        particularly the sin of adultery.

He knew that she could never totally eliminate sin
    but she certainly could overcome the one sin
        that truly weighed her down;
            the one sin that kept her
                from living as a child of God.

Once she was liberated from that bondage,
    she was freed to really love and be loved
        and it was a love that didn't stop her from kneeling
        down and washing Jesus' feet.

She learned the symbolism of washing feet
    long before Jesus taught it to His disciples.

    "If I, therefore your master and teacher have washed your
    feet, you ought to wash one another's feet" (John 13:14).

Humility is a key to salvation.

Humility leads us to admitting we are sinners
    which opens the door to reconciliation and forgiveness.

Find the grace to admit you are a sinner.

Return to God and seek the forgiveness that only God can give.

Forgive others, forget the past
        and then go on with your life as a forgiver and a lover.

CHAPTER SEVEN

A Little Bit of Heaven on the Way to Heaven

Now one of the criminals hanging there reviled Jesus, saying, "Are you not the Messiah? Save yourself and us." The other, however, rebuking him, said in reply, "Have you no fear of God, for you are subject to the same condemnation? And, indeed, we have been condemned justly, for the sentence we received correlates to our crimes, but this man has done nothing criminal." Then he said, "Jesus, remember me when you come into your kingdom." He replied to him, "Amen, I say to you, today you will be with me in Paradise (Luke 24:39-43).

"Today you will be with me in Paradise."

This conversation between the criminal and Jesus has always intrigued me.

As a Catholic I was taught that
>we had to go to purgatory as a punishment due to sin;
>>the worse the sin the longer the sentence.

The man on the cross is often called the "Good Thief"
>but before his confession he was anything but good.

He admits he deserves his punishment
>which means he was most likely a murderer.

He was probably an insurrectionist who had killed many.

But notice he never says he's sorry.

There's no act of contrition here;
>no promise that he will never sin again,

>just the recognition that Jesus is innocent;
>>the recognition that Jesus is no ordinary man.

A simple statement,

>"Lord, remember me when you come into your kingdom."

An amazing response,

>"Amen, I say to you, today you will be with me in Paradise."

Paradise!

That's the same as heaven, right?

Just what is heaven?

>A place above the clouds?

>Another dimension on the other side of a worm hole?

No one really knows
>but I think it's safe to say that heaven is a place
>>where God lives;
>>>a place where God is.

It's the place where God reigns.

>It's the Kingdom of God.

But Jesus says,

>". . . the Kingdom of God is near" (Lk 21:31).

He even says,

>". . . the Kingdom of God has come upon you" (Lk 11:20).

So the Kingdom of God or the Kingdom of Heaven,
    which seem to be interchangeable,
        is in our midst and
            it's the place where we find God

That means that God is near to us here on earth
    and we need to find Him here
        if we want to know what heaven is like.

The truth is if we haven't found God here on earth
    we'll never find Him in heaven.

How can we possibly recognize God in the next life
    if we don't recognize Him in this life?

The way to recognize God in this life is to recognize Jesus.

    "Now this is eternal life, that they should know you
    the only true God and the one whom you sent,
    Jesus Christ" (John 17:3).

Jesus reveals the Father and brings us to Him.

If we know Jesus in this life
    we will know the Father in this life
        and to experience God is heaven.

So heaven is not some place beyond the stars.

It's not some eternal resort or island paradise where we go to for some R and R.

Heaven is already in our midst!

We don't go to heaven;
    we're already experiencing it!

A friend of mine often says,

> "We're having a little bit of heaven on the way to heaven."

Earth has to be the place where heaven begins.

Otherwise, why are we here?

What's the point?

Our life here on earth has to have meaning and purpose.

But it's not just a brief stay on the way to eternity.

God brought us into this world so
    we could experience what
        it's like in the next world.

It's the very first place where we begin to experience eternity.

It's the first place
    we begin to experience things
        that really matter;
            things that will last forever.

It's the first place we experience beauty, music, art
    and, most of all, loving relationships.

It's a place where love is
    and love is of heaven
        and God is love!

> "God is love and whoever remains in love, remains in God and God in him" (1 John 4:16).

Have you ever experienced the love of God?

If you have,
> then you've already experienced
>> a little bit of heaven on the way to heaven.

Heaven is about love.

If we have never loved
> then we have never experienced heaven.

But the majority of us know
> what it is to love and be loved
>> so we're already in heaven!

Don't wait for it to come ten, twenty or forty years from now.

Celebrate the fact
> that eternal life began the moment you were conceived.

Yet, don't take it for granted.

We're here for a reason.

That reason is found in Christ.

The fact that God became a human person,
> lived among us, died, rose from the dead
>> and ascended provides the reason.

In and through the life of Christ
> God showed us our destiny.

By revealing Himself to us as a human being
> God is telling us that our flesh is sanctified.

> It is not mortal but immortal.

Christ's resurrection reminds us
>> that death doesn't end in the grave,
>>> His ascension that our flesh is transformed into spirit.

And, because Jesus Himself became pure spirit,
>> He remains with us forever
>>> just as we will remain forever in the Spirit.

"But," you ask, "what about little children who die, and those who die in childbirth or those who are aborted."

"How can they experience a little heaven on the way to heaven?"

Do you think God doesn't have a plan for them?

Do you think they are forgotten or that God sticks them in Limbo or some other place invented by Theologians?

God knew and loved them before they were born.

> "Before you were formed in the womb I knew you;
> before you were born I dedicated you . . ." (Jer 1:5).

God has a plan which is far better
>> than any we could ever think of.

Let God take care of it
>> and concentrate on what needs to be done here on earth.

It amazes me that,
>> while everyone was thinking about going to heaven,
>>> God was thinking about coming to earth!

This wretched place filled with war, disease, death and destruction.

Why is this place so wretched?

Because there is not enough love, that's why.

Jesus came, i.e. God came,
        to teach us how to love.

        "Love one another as I have loved you" (John 15:12).

So we must be imitators of Christ.

The more we are like Him the more we love.

The more we love the more we experience heaven.

Hellooo? Are you listening?

Some will say,

        "What about people who live in third world nations, people who are starving or dying from disease?"

        "Don't tell me they're experiencing a little bit of heaven on the way to heaven."

Well, if they are experiencing love,
        if they know what it means to love,
            then, yes they are.

And if they're not then shame on us!

If they're not being loved or expressing love
        then it's our responsibility to see to it they are.

That's the Gospel
        and if we believe in the Gospel
            then we need to preach it-
                "to the ends of the earth".

We need to tell people about Jesus and His love for us.

We need to demonstrate our love for God and mankind
    by loving others as Jesus loves us.

We are able to do this
    because we know we have been loved.

We know God loves us
    and so we able to love
        because we were first loved by God.

With His love God empowers us to love others
    with the only kind of love that really matters-
        divine love.

What is divine love?

It's not about feelings or emotions.

It's not a nice warm fuzzy feeling inside.

Divine love is to love as God loves.

It's loving your enemies,
    praying for your persecutors;
        wanting what's best for others
            even when they hate you!

It's a love that doesn't retaliate with
    an "eye for an eye" or
        a "tooth for a tooth".

It's never judging and ALWAYS forgiving.

Have you ever read the Sermon on the Mount (Matt 5-7)?

It's all in there.

Read it.
Let its teaching sink in
    and become an integral part of who you are
        and you'll know what divine love is.

God, through Jesus, is trying to show us how to love
    and we turn the tables on God
        by applying our behavior to Him.

God is a judge, we say.

God gets even.

God retaliates.

God basically does everything we do but on a grand scale.

Think about this a minute.

Matthew 5:48 tells us to
    "be perfect even as your heavenly Father is perfect."

In other words, we must be like God as much as we possibly can.

So, if Jesus tells us we must never judge others
    how can we portray God as judgmental?

If Jesus tells us we must forgive others
    how can we possibly think that God will not forgive others?

If we're not allowed to get even,
    never to strike another when struck (Matt 5:39)
    how can we picture God striking us down with natural
    disasters, and killing tens of thousands of people
        because they were sinners?

Yet we do.

The self-righteousness in us does it all the time.
We love to play God—the God we've invented!

The problem is the God so many of us have invented
        has little or nothing to do with love.

Divine love simply wants what's best for another,
        regardless of whom that other person is.

And you don't have to like someone to love him or her!

I may not like some of my relatives
        but I still want what's best for them-
                to be blest with health and happiness.

I certainly would never wish bad things for them.

Yet, how many people in this world hate some of their relatives?

They even hate people they don't know.

How many times have you heard people
        say they hate a politician, an athlete or a movie star?

How can you hate someone you've never even met?

Yet people do and they still dare to call themselves Christian!

    "Whoever hates his brother is a murderer" (1 John 3:15).

Murderers are not of God.

Do these people really hear the Gospel?

They may have read the Sermon on the Mount
        but they've never really heard it!

    "Pray for those who persecute you" (Matt 5:44).

Of all these people you hate,
    I bet none of them are persecuting you.

Shouldn't you be praying for them instead of hating them?

If we are really going to enjoy a little bit of heaven
    on the way to heaven
        then we have to allow God to love us
           and then love as God loves.

The more we do that the happier we are.

But, it's not as important to love God
    as it is to love your neighbor.

I say this because you can pretend to love God
    and get away with it
        but you can never do that with people.

Your true colors will shine.

In fact, you cannot love God without loving your neighbor.

    "If anyone says, 'I love God' but hates his brother,
    he is a liar" (1 John 4:20).

Christianity is the only religion I know that is not God centered.

It is people centered.

Read the Gospels.

How many times does Jesus focus on loving God,
    pleasing God or serving God?

Very few!

Yet over and over again He tells us to love our neighbor,

    to love them as a He loves us.

Over and over again He tells us

    to forgive others,

    be kind to others,

    to serve others,

    to wash their feet,

    to make peace with our enemies,

    to care for the oppressed,

    and to visit the sick

Over and over again He tells stories about

    good Samaritans,

    loving fathers

    and generous employers.

How many times does He Himself heal others and forgive others?

I wonder how many more stories about
    good thieves and adulterous women there were
        that the Gospels didn't record.

The message in the Gospels is clear.

The way in which we

    serve God,

    love God

    and honor God

is how much we

    serve,

    love

    and honor

our fellow men and women.

Remember the story in Matt 25:31-45 where Christ returns to judge the nations?

He separates the sheep and the goats, the good and the bad.

What were the criteria He used to separate them?

> "When I was hungry you gave me to eat,
> thirsty and you gave me to drink,
> a stranger and you welcomed me,
> naked and you clothed me,
> ill and you cared for me,
> in prison and you visited me." (Matt 25:35-36)

Does He say anything about

    how many times we went to Church,

    how much we put in the collection basket,

    how many novenas we said or

    how many times we received communion?

It's not that those aren't important
> but they are only important
>> if they lead us to care for the
>>> oppressed, the needy and the lost.

If we haven't done that then we've missed the point.

And the point is,

> ". . . what you did not do for one of these least ones,
> you did not do for me. And these will go off to eternal
> punishment, and the righteous to eternal life." (Matt 25:45)

In fact, if you read the story carefully
> you find that He's not just talking about believers.

> It's about *everyone* who cares and *everyone* who loves
>> because when we love others we love God.

Jesus wants us to understand
> that's where our joy is
>> and our fulfillment as human beings.

It's our resurrection from the deadness of a hard heart.

It's our ascension into heaven!

It's how we enjoy a little bit of heaven on the way to heaven.

CPSIA information can be obtained at www.ICGtesting.com
Printed in the USA
BVOW080450091012
302479BV00005B/5/P